WELCOME TO THE MOON

AND OTHER PLAYS

BY JOHN PATRICK SHANLEY

★

★

DRAMATISTS
PLAY SERVICE
INC.

WELCOME TO THE MOON, and the other plays in this volume, were first presented by The Ensemble Studio Theatre, in New York City, in the fall of 1982. They were directed by Douglas Aibel; scenic design was by Evelyn Sakash; costume design was by Michele Reisch; lighting design was by Mal Sturchio; sound design was by Bruce Ellman; the music director was Barry Koron; and the production stage manager was Teresa Elwert.

The company was as follows:

Robert Joy	Anne O'Sullivan
John Henry Kurtz	James Ryan
Michael Albert Mantel	June Stein

These plays are dedicated to James Ryan, for his friendship.

CONTENTS

AUTHOR'S NOTE

I just thought I'd include a little note about how to do these little plays. Keep it innocent and simple. For THE RED COAT, all that's needed is a small bench that seats two; in LET US GO OUT INTO THE STARRY NIGHT, two little cafe tables and one chair at each table. When the woman decides to join the man at his table, she can bring her own chair along. The ghosts and monsters mentioned in this piece can be managed with simple puppets or masks. The stars and planets drop that's called for near the conclusion *should* have a homemade quality. If you don't want to deal with a dropcloth, you can probably achieve an adequate effect with a slide projector. In OUT WEST the cowboys shouldn't use guns that look at all real; it might be best if they just mime them.

If you decide to do more than one of these plays, or all of them, the order can be switched around to suit you, but you would be wise, I think, to do WELCOME TO THE MOON last. It just feels right that way; and also, since it requires the most in the way of props and such, you probably won't want to deal with a scene change after that.

If you're looking for a way to link the pieces together, music works pretty well, either recorded, or a live pianist who is visible but not onstage. Slides can be fun, too. Romantic pictures and romantic airs.

Finally, just a word about acting style. Some of this stuff would be pretty easy to camp up, but trust me, it doesn't work well that way. I wrote it from my heart, and it acts best the same way.

THE RED COAT

THE RED COAT

Night time on a side street. A street light shines down on some steps through a green tree. Moonlight mixes in the shadows. A seventeen year-old boy sits on the steps in a white shirt with a loosened skinny tie, black dress pants, and black shoes. He is staring off. His eyes are shining. A sixteen year-old girl enters, in neighborhood party clothes: short skirt, blouse, penny loafers.

JOHN. Hi, Mary.
MARY. Oh! I didn't see you there. You're hiding.
JOHN. Not from you, Mary.
MARY. Who from?
JOHN. Oh, nobody. I was up at Susan's party.
MARY. That's where I'm going.
JOHN. Oh.
MARY. Why did you leave?
JOHN. No reason.
MARY. You just gonna sit here?
JOHN. For awhile.
MARY. Well, I'm going in.
JOHN. Oh. Okay . . . Oh! I'm not going in . . . I mean came out because . . . Oh, go in!
MARY. What's wrong with you, John?
JOHN. I left the party because you weren't there. That's why I left the party.
MARY. Why'd ya leave the party 'cause I wasn't there?
JOHN. I dunno.
MARY. I'm going in.
JOHN. I left the party 'cause I felt like everything I wanted was outside the party . . . out here. There's a breeze out here, and the moon . . . look at the way the moon is . . . and I knew you were outside somewhere, too! So I came out and sat on the steps here and I thought that maybe you'd come and I would be here . . . outside the party, on the steps, in the moonlight . . . and those other people . . . the ones at the party . . . wouldn't be here . . . but the night would be here . . . and you and me would be talking on the steps in the night in the moonlight and I could tell you . . .

MARY. Tell me what?
JOHN. How I feel!
MARY. How you feel about what?
JOHN. I don't know. I was looking out the window at the party . . . and I drank some wine . . . and I was looking out the window at the moon and I thought of you . . . and I could feel my heart . . . breaking.
MARY. Joh . . .
JOHN. I felt that wine and the moon and your face all pushing in my heart and I left the party and I came out here.
MARY. Your eyes are all shiny.
JOHN. I know. And I came out here looking for the moon and I saw that street light shining down through the leaves of that tree.
MARY. Hey yeah! It does look pretty.
JOHN. It's beautiful. I didn't know a street light could be beautiful. I've always thought of them as being cold and blue, you know? But this one's yellow . . . and it comes down through the leaves and the leaves are so green! Mary, I love you!
MARY. Oh!
JOHN. I shouldn't 've said it. I shouldn't 've said it.
MARY. No, no. That's all right.
JOHN. My heart's breaking. You must think I'm so stupid . . . but I can feel it breaking. I wish I could stop talking. I can't. I can't.
MARY. I never heard you talking like this before.
JOHN. That's 'cause this is outside the party and it's night and there's a moon up there . . . and a street light that's more beautiful than the sun! My God, the sidewalk's beautiful. Those bits of shiny stuff in the concrete . . . look how they're sparkling up the light!
MARY. You're crying! You're crying over the sidewalk!
JOHN. I love you, Mary!
MARY. That's all right. But don't cry over the sidewalk. You're usually so quiet.
JOHN. Okay. Okay. (*A pause. Then John grabs Mary and kisses her.*)
MARY. Oh . . . you used your tongue. (*He kisses her again.*) You . . . should we go into the party?
JOHN. No.
MARY. I got all dressed . . . I tasted the wine on your . . . mouth. You were waiting for me out here? I wasn't even going

to come. I don't like Susan so much. I was going to stay home and watch a movie. What would you have done?

JOHN. I don't know. (*Kisses her again. She kisses him back.*)

MARY. You go to St. Nicholas of Tolentine, don't you?

JOHN. Yeah.

MARY. I see you on the platform on a hundred and forty-ninth street sometimes.

JOHN. I see you, too! Sometimes I just let the trains go by until the last minute, hoping to see you.

MARY. Really?

JOHN. Yeah.

MARY. I take a look around for you but I always get on my train. What would you have done if I hadn't come?

JOHN. I don't know. Walked around. I walk around a lot.

MARY. Walk around where?

JOHN. I walk around your block a lot. Sometimes I run into you.

MARY. You mean that was *planned*? Wow! I always thought you were coming from somewhere.

JOHN. I love you, Mary. I can't believe I'm saying it . . . to you . . . out loud. I love you.

MARY. Kiss me again. (*They kiss.*)

JOHN. I've loved you for a long time.

MARY. How long?

JOHN. Months. Remember that big snowball fight?

MARY. In the park?

JOHN. Yeah. That's when it was. That's when I fell in love with you. You were wearing a red coat.

MARY. Oh, that coat! I've had that for ages and ages. I've had it since the sixth grade.

JOHN. Really?

MARY. I have really special feelings for that coat. I feel like it's part of me . . . like it stands for something . . . my childhood . . . something like that.

JOHN. You look nice in that coat. I think I sensed something about it . . . the coat . . . it's special to me, too. It's so good to be able to talk to you like this.

MARY. Yeah, this is nice. That's funny how you felt that about my coat. The red one. No one knows how I feel about that coat.

JOHN. I think I do, Mary.

MARY. Do you? If you understood about my red coat . . . that red coat is like all the good things about when I was a kid . . . it's like I still have all the good kid things when I'm in that red coat . . . it's like being grown up and having your childhood, too. You know what it's like? It's like being in one of those movies where you're safe, even when you're in an adventure. Do you know what I mean? Sometimes, in a movie the hero's doin' all this stuff that's dangerous, but you know, becausa the kind of movie it is, that he's not gonna get hurt. Bein' in that red coat is like that . . . like bein' safe in an adventure.

JOHN. And that's the way you were in that snowball fight! It was like you knew that nothing could go wrong!

MARY. That's right! That's right! That's the way it feels! Oh, you do understand! It seems silly but I've always wanted someone to understand some things and that was one of them . . . the red coat.

JOHN. I do understand! I do!

MARY. I don't know. I don't know. I don't know about tomorrow, but . . . right this minute I . . . love you!

JOHN. Oh, Mary!

MARY. Oh, kiss me, John. Please!

JOHN. You're crying!

MARY. I didn't know. I didn't know two people could understand some things . . . share some things. (*They kiss.*)

JOHN. It must be terrible not to.

MARY. What?

JOHN. Be able to share things.

MARY. It is! It is! But don't you remember? Only a few minutes ago we were alone. I feel like I could tell you anything. Isn't that crazy?

JOHN. Do you want to go for a walk?

MARY. No, no. Let's stay right here. Between the streetlight and the moon. Under the tree. Tell me that you love me.

JOHN. I love you.

MARY. I love you, too. You're good-looking, did you know that? Does your mother tell you that?

JOHN. Yeah, she does.

MARY. Your eyes are shining.

JOHN. I know. I can feel them shining.

The Lights Go Down Slowly

DOWN AND OUT

DOWN AND OUT

Love, a woman in a shawl full of holes, stands at a table. On the table is a large candle burning brightly, and a red box. A distant storm rages without. Love is setting the table. There are two spoons and one paper napkin. Carefully, with trembling hands, she tears the napkin in half, and puts one half at each place. A knock at the door.

LOVE. Is that you, Poet? (*Enter the Poet, in wet yellow rain gear.*)
POET. It is I, my Love.
LOVE. How did you fare?
POET. Not well. (*He coughs.*)
LOVE. Still sick?
POET. Worse. Though still, it is nothing.
LOVE. You must rest.
POET. Yes. And yet, there is no possibility of rest.
LOVE. The book then, that you wanted, you could not get it?
POET. The library was closed. The library used to be open at all times, but then less and less. Now it is open one half hour a week.
LOVE. What has happened to the world?
POET. Cutbacks.
LOVE. Cutbacks.
POET. The painters in the parks are bags of bones, the clowns are tired, the tragedians have succumbed to pettiness, and the poets . . . What's for dinner?
LOVE. Water and beans.
POET. Again?
LOVE. Yes.
POET. Six days now we have eaten water and beans.
LOVE. Yes.
POET. And yet, still the water is sweet.
LOVE. It is.
POET. And still the beans are the true fruit of the earth.
LOVE. I love you.
POET. And you are my love. Is it safe in the box?
LOVE. It is safe. (*Violent knocking at the door. The door swings open. A shrouded Figure stands on the threshold.*)

FIGURE. (*In a ghastly whisper.*) Are you the Poet?
POET. I am.
FIGURE. Give here your library card.
LOVE. No! You can't take his library card! He's sick! He has no money! He eats nothing but beans! The library card is all he has!
FIGURE. Give here your library card. (*The Poet gives the Figure his card and stands away. The door shuts. The Figure laughs madly from off. The laughter trails away.*)
POET. They have silenced the song of Shakespeare. They forbid me the comfort of Keats.
LOVE. Don't despond, my Poet. Though they have taken everything from you, and you are not well, don't despond.
POET. It is not for these things I despond, my Love. As you well know. But because I cannot write.
LOVE. But you can!
POET. No.
LOVE. But I know you can! There are a hundred songs I see in you.
POET. Yes. That is true. But I cannot write them. Because I have no pencil.
LOVE. It will come!
POET. I wait. Every day. I have put my soul away against the time. But the postman comes, and then he goes again. And no pencil.
LOVE. It will come!
POET. Let's eat.
LOVE. All right. (*Violent knocking at the door. It opens. A shrouded Figure holding a huge amount of money.*)
FIGURE. (*In a ghastly whisper.*) Money! Money! Money!
LOVE. Look at all the money!
POET. How wonderful!
LOVE. Look at how green it is! How green!
POET. It's beautiful! Can I have it?
FIGURE. Give me your soul. Give me your soul.
POET. (*Picks up the red box.*) My soul?
LOVE. NEVER! GET OUT GET OUT GET OUT! (*The door slams. Mad laughter trailing away.*)
POET. My soul? Why would they want my soul?

LOVE. You are a child. I forget sometimes. These days you are a child.
POET. I remember when the wolf was at the door, and I was not afraid.
LOVE. Eat your beans.
POET. Yes, I must eat my beans. I feel weak.
LOVE. Tomorrow I must sell this table. We must learn to eat without a table.
POET. Whatever is necessary. I'm sorry. I'm sorry I ever wrote a poem.
LOVE. Don't say that.
POET. But I am. I am silly and I have failed. No one wants my poetry. The man in the newspaper said I am an untalented fool. The man in the newspaper was right. We are alone. Unknown. We live on beans. They have taken my library card. And I have no pencil. (*A civilized knock on the door. The door opens. It's the Postman. He has a small package.*)
POSTMAN. Package for the Poet.
LOVE. (*Taking it.*) Thank you. (*Postman exits.*) It's your pencil. It's come. (*He takes it from her, trembling. He unwraps it gently. It's broken.*)
POET. It's broken.
LOVE. Oh. (*He breaks down and weeps.*) So, it has come. I have kept this key around my neck against this day, my Poet. For you are my love and I am your Love. The darkest thing has come, and led to a moment of despair. But look! See here! I am your Love who has never left you! I can turn a tiny lock and open up your soul again! (*She opens the box, which is his soul. It plays music. The Poet is bathed in a powerful light. He rises up.*)
POET. I will sharpen this broken pencil and I will write a line of poetry! And I will learn to eat without a table!
LOVE. Yes! Yes! (*A wolf howls without.*) Poet! Poet! The Wolf! The Wolf is at the door!
POET. I am not afraid. (*The lights depart.*)

PROPERTY LIST

Table
Candle, in candlestick
Red box (music box)
Spoons (2)
Paper napkin
Library card (Poet)
Bundle of money (Figure)
Small package, containing pencil (Postman)

LET US GO OUT INTO THE STARRY NIGHT

LET US GO OUT INTO THE STARRY NIGHT

A cafe. Two tables. At the table L., *sits a tormented young man surrounded by ghosts and monsters. They chew on his head, claw his stomach, whisper in his ear. He stares off, sipping a glass of wine. At the table* R., *sits a skinny earnest woman, and her girlfriend, who is a dummy.*

WOMAN. Don't envy me because I'm skinny. I know you don't really, but you do say you do, which bothers me. If you knew why I was skinny . . . I'm going to tell you why I'm skinny. I can't find nourishment. I'm not talking about food now, which I think you guessed. I'm talking about the world. The world does not nourish me. At least at the moment. Do you know what I'm talking about? You don't know. You don't have any idea. And the reason you're ignorant—because that's what you are, really—is that you don't care. If you cared, you would know what I'm talking about. Or, at least, I would find your stupidity more endearing. Because it would be stupidity of the head, which can be easily forgiven. But what you have—and it's very common and unforgivable—what you have is stupidity of the heart. (*All goes dark but for a spot on the woman.*) Why am I sitting here with this woman who does not love me? I am squandering something on this woman. An important energy of which I only have a certain amount, maybe. When I should be talking to that young man, at that table yonder. He looks like Dostoevsky. I'm not speaking cosmetically now. I mean he really looks like Dostoevsky. Time for resolve. For courage. I'm going to approach him. Make up an excuse to get away from the table. (*Lights up again. She picks up a glass of water from the table and pours it over her head.*) Oh, excuse me. I seem to have spilled some water on my head. I'll be right back. (*She goes to the young man's table.*) Hello, you don't know me, but could I borrow a cigarette never mind I don't smoke. I must look terrible. My hair's wet and you don't care, do you? I can tell. You're not concerned

with outward appearance. What are these things that are bothering you? I can see them, even if no one else can.
MAN. Ghosts and monsters.
WOMAN. You have a lot of them.
MAN. Yes.
WOMAN. Are you lonely?
MAN. I'm terribly lonely.
WOMAN. So am I.
MAN. It's hopeless.
WOMAN. Why?
MAN. Too many problems.
WOMAN. I have problems, too.
MAN. I know. I can see that.
WOMAN. But you know why we're suffering? We're suffering because we are in direct contact with our lives. I can't believe that that's a bad thing. I'm skinny because my body honestly reflects my soul, which is famished. Listen, I must talk to you.
MAN. Do you want to talk to me seriously?
WOMAN. Yes. Exactly. I want to have a serious conversation with you. (*The ghosts and monsters stop working on the young man.*)
MAN. That makes them quiet. They respect serious conversation. In fact, they contribute to a serious conversation.
WOMAN. Give me one minute to deal with matters mundane. I've got to get rid of my friend. No. I only want to do meaningful, truthful things now. I won't lie to her. I will make this a great act. An important moment in my life. (*Addresses the dummy.*) This supposed friendship between us has been an unconscionable lie. It symbolizes for me a lot of friendships I have had with soulless people who sneer at sincerity and honest intellectual pursuit. I hereby end all such friendships. Service! (*A box flies on from offstage. She grabs the dummy, chucks it in the box, nails the lid with great efficiency, slaps a sticker on the side that reads "Irrelevant," and boots the box offstage. She returns to the young man.*) Which one is that there? My God, she's ugly.
MAN. That's the ghost of my mother.
WOMAN. Was she really that ugly?
MAN. Oh no. She was just ordinary looking.
WOMAN. Then why does her ghost look so vicious?
MAN. She doesn't look too bad today really. Some nights she visits me looking like a rotting side of beef and carrying a big

knife in her hand. When the woman was alive, she bossed me around a lot, so now that she's dead, she's an ugly ghost. It's very neat, really. If you brood about these things enough, it all gets very neat. The ghost of my mother that I have made is ugly. Her revenge on me is to frighten me with her ugliness.

WOMAN. It's a relief to talk to a man like you.

MAN. You're looking for romance?

WOMAN. Yes.

MAN. It's hopeless.

WOMAN. But you are lonely?

MAN. Terribly.

WOMAN. Then you should share with me what torments you, and I will help you find peace.

MAN. What's in it for you?

WOMAN. Seriousness. I need to be serious. I'm tired of taking things lightly. Do you believe in God?

MAN. No. But I do feel there is a spirituality in the world.

WOMAN. Yes, so do I! I think that everything in nature and in psychology is explainable, predictable, and that that's incredible! Where does all that logic come from? Imagine a mind big enough to contain all this logic around us. Maybe it's the mind of God, I don't know. What a relief to say these things even if they're sophomoric. I think there's a sophomore in a lot of people, just waiting to get out.

MAN. I have tried to live with women. I have tried to have women for friends. It never works. It always ends up very painful.

WOMAN. Of course it was painful. To live, to honestly live, is very painful. My sister has never lived. She denies her ghosts and monsters, even though they're the most interesting thing about her. She distracts herself by cleaning things and having babies. The point I was about to make isn't true. I was about to say that my sister, because she doesn't confront life, isn't in pain. But she is. Of course she is. She's in agony. The difference between you and her is that she's in dumb agony. She doesn't admit to it, and her heart is stupid about it. So I guess the point is that everything is painful, so why not be honest about the pain?

MAN. I feel better. When I first saw you, you looked like everyone else. But now I can see that you are beautiful.

WOMAN. There is a special light on you, I think.
MAN. It's coming from your eyes.
WOMAN. We've reached it. Come with me. Let us go out into the starry night. (*A drop of stars and planets unrolls with a thud.*)
MAN. You're not as you were before.
WOMAN. Neither are you. Your ghosts and monsters are gone.
MAN. Look at the sky. The stars and planets. It's beyond belief that such beauty could exist. And yet we go for years and never see it.
WOMAN. I wanted to travel through the universe and meet other beings.
MAN. That was my dream!
WOMAN. Tonight I feel as if that dream has been fulfilled.
MAN. How can we bring each other such joy? And it seems so easy. The stars and planets are always up there, aren't they?
WOMAN. Yes.
MAN. And people are always lonely, aren't they?
WOMAN. Yes.
MAN. And we have this potential, which I feel tonight, for the first time in so many years, this potential for joy.
WOMAN. Champagne. (*They make a popping sound, finger in mouth.*) It's delicious.
MAN. It tastes like I'm drinking little sparks.
WOMAN. I'm alive. There are tears in my eyes. Kiss me. (*They don't kiss, but it's as if they have.*)
MAN. Why can't I stay here?
WOMAN. Don't think about it.
MAN. How did we get here? Maybe if I knew how we got here, I could find my way back here again.
WOMAN. Stars and planets.
MAN. How did we get here?
WOMAN. We got here by being serious. (*They reach toward each other. The lights fade.*)

THE END

PROPERTY LIST

Chairs (2)
Tables (2)
Glass of wine
Glass of water
Female dummy
Large Box (to fit dummy)
Sticker, with IRRELEVANT on it

OUT WEST

OUT WEST

The sound of wind blowing. The lights reveal a Cowboy.

COWBOY. O, I love the land when it's livin', the heart when it's young, the wind when it's blowin', the campfire, out on the praire night, and the stars all bright, but small and many, like a busted-ta-bits-moon! I say that I am a free man, and the water in the lake, and the animals on the shore, and the mountain men who live in caves like holy saints or bears say back to me again that I am a free man. Hallelujah! (*The lights reveal a Girl.*)

GIRL. I am a girl. I live in a coffin called a room. I live in a tomb called a house. I live in a graveyard called a town, with fathers and cousins and mothers and uncles and brothers and aunts and sisters, like cold dead key-clutchin' jailers; but I have a window, and I have seen the stars, and far fires on praire nights, and wild men singin' in the dark—Cowboys they call them—and I have pressed my soul to the glass so that it may have sight, and I have fixed my heart with a star like a pin to the bosom of the night, so that my heart is not in me, but out upon the Wild West! And that is why, even though I am a slave and I am dead, something of me is free, too. Something of me is altogether free!

COWBOY. Look upon me, young girl, prisoner of the town. Look upon me and know there is another way to be, another mind to think other thoughts, another heart to beat, another soul to fly out into the hub of the Wild West! Look upon me and know that I am a free man! I am a Cowboy!

GIRL. Hallelujah!

COWBOY. And can you see me as I am?

GIRL. I can see you, Mister. (*Enter Betsy, a dance hall girl.*)

BETSY. I can see you, too, Mister.

COWBOY. Who are you?

BETSY. My name's Betsy. I'm a dance hall girl. Can I buy you a drink?

COWBOY. You sure can, honey.

GIRL. No, no. Don't.

COWBOY. What's this?

GIRL. You shouldn't drink, and you shouldn't talk to girls like her.
COWBOY. Well now, why shouldn't I?
BETSY. Because she has her own ideas 'bout what a Cowboy is.
GIRL. You are special. You are pure. You are a dream. You have lived like a priest under the prairie moon. Don't let the town spoil you.
COWBOY. I reckon I'll have a drink. (*The Girl runs out, crying. The wind stops blowing.*)
BETSY. Well, she's a tender thing, ain't she?
COWBOY. She could only see one part of me.
BETSY. Barkeep! (*Enter the Barkeep. A saloon piano starts up.*)
BARKEEP. Yes, Betsy?
BETSY. Whiskey for me and the Cowboy.
BARKEEP. Sure thing, Betsy. You gonna get him drunk and promise him upstairs, then steal his money and leave him just a broken-hearted fool?
BETSY. Naw, Pete. I'll get him drunk and promise him upstairs, all right. But this is a real Cowboy, just in from the mystery of the Wild West. I'll promise him upstairs and I'll give him upstairs. And then he'll leave me, though I begged him to stay, and I gave him all my money, and I'll be the broken-hearted fool.
BARKEEP. Here's your whiskey. Have you ever killed a man?
COWBOY. Yes, I have killed a man.
BETSY. Down the hatch, pardner.
BARKEEP. Who was it?
COWBOY. Stagecoach Johnny. (*Enter Stagecoach Johnny's brother, his gun drawn.*)
BROTHER. Did I hear you say you killed Stagecoach Johnny?
COWBOY. That's what I said. Who are you?
BROTHER. I'm his brother. Stand up.
COWBOY. I ain't got no quarrel with you, pardner.
BROTHER. You killed my brother didn't ya? Stand up. (*Enter Girl, at a run.*)
GIRL. No, no. You can't fight!
BROTHER. Get outta here, Sally!
GIRL. I tell you ya can't draw on him, Billy! He hasn't gotta chance. You'll kill him!
BROTHER. You're talkin' like you're sweet on him.

GIRL. Sweet on him? No, I don't care nothin' about him. He's just some saddle bum who drinks whiskeys in the saloon and fools with cheap women.

BETSY. Who you callin' cheap!

COWBOY. Hush, Betsy. Let's keep the women outta this.

BROTHER. That's all right by me. Sally, get outta here.

BARKEEP. Yeah, come on missy. I'll walk ya to your carriage.

GIRL. I'm not leavin'! O, dammit Cowboy, Billy was right. I am sweet on you.

BROTHER. First you killed my brother, and now y'ar stealin' my girl! Get outta the way, Sally!

COWBOY. He's right. You'd better move outta the way. This fella means ta draw on me.

GIRL. I won't, I tell you! I won't!

BROTHER. Pete, get her outta the way.

BARKEEP. Alright missy, why don't you jus' come on outside with me. (*They move to door, but go no further. Piano stops.*)

BROTHER. Now its just you and me.

BETSY. Wait a minute!

BROTHER. What in thunder do you want?

BETSY. (*Kisses Cowboy.*) Now just wait a minute. (*Takes off garter.*)

COWBOY. What are you doin', Betsy?

BETSY. (*Giving him the garter.*) Keep this in your pocket for luck. I'll be upstairs . . . waitin'. Come on up after the fight.

BROTHER. Hey Betsy, I'm the one who's gonna win this here shootin' match.

BETSY. (*To Cowboy.*) I'll be upstairs. First door on your right. Don't bother to knock. (*Betsy exits.*)

COWBOY. Let's get this over with.

BROTHER. That suits me fine. Draw on the count a three. You count, Pete.

BARKEEP. I don't wanna count.

BROTHER. Well, you jus' go ahead and count anyway.

BARKEEP. Okay. One, two . . . (*The Brother begins to draw on the count of two. The Girl breaks away from the Barkeep.*)

GIRL. No, no, don't kill him! (*She throws herself in front of the Cowboy and is shot. The Cowboy shoots the Brother.*)

COWBOY. You shouldn't have done that.

GIRL. I have been living in my room all my life waiting for the

world ta notice me. I have been a slave to my parents. The only dreams I had were from lookin' out at the praire. I never was alive until I saw you. At least now I'm dyin' after I was alive.
COWBOY. Poor little thing. She's dead.
BARKEEP. (*Checking the Brother.*) So's this one. He started drawin' his gun when I was countin' two. She saved your life, Mister.
COWBOY. I know.
BARKEEP. Well, I reckon you'll be goin' up ta see Betsy now. She's waitin' for ya.
COWBOY. Naw, I think I'd better be goin' along now.
BARKEEP. What'll I tell Betsy?
COWBOY. I reckon you can tell her I'm joinin' up with the wagon train. I'm goin further West.
BARKEEP. She ain't gonna like it none.
COWBOY. Well, I guess there ain't nothin' I can do about that. I'm a Cowboy. (*The Cowboy, whistling one of the old Cowboy tunes, slowly exits.*)

PROPERTY LIST

Pistol (Stagecoach Johnny's brother)
Garter (Betsy)

A LONELY IMPULSE OF DELIGHT

A LONELY IMPULSE OF DELIGHT

Night time. Two guys, Jim and Walter, are crouched at the edge of a lake. Light from the water makes patterns on their faces.

JIM. What are we doing out here, Walter?
WALTER. Shh. Just keep your eyes open, all right?
JIM. All right, Walter. But what are we doing out here?
WALTER. Come on now, don't get boring, Jim. You came, and I thank you that you came. Now relax. And keep your eyes open.
JIM. But what am I looking for?
WALTER. Never mind and just trust me and look!
JIM. I'm not into blind faith. It doesn't appeal to me.
WALTER. You're my best friend in the world, Jim. If there's anybody who understands me it's you. If there's anybody I trust it's you. That's why you're here. Because you're my best friend in the world.
JIM. I'm sitting at a nice silly party. I'm about to get somewhere with a nice silly woman. And my friend Walter takes me by the arm, and leads me to Central Park Lake.
WALTER. It's pretty. Enjoy it.
JIM. It's two o'clock in the morning.
WALTER. Two-ten. Listen. How quiet. "And the spirit of God moved upon the face of the waters."
JIM. Look at that duck. It's asleep. It's mouth's hanging open.
WALTER. Did you ever have a dream? Something in your head. A feeling. Something you wanted but you knew you could never have?
JIM. Probably. But nothing comes to mind.
WALTER. Something's happened to me, Jim. Something that could never happen has happened to me. And it's the most wonderful thing. And the saddest. And nobody knows.
JIM. All right, I'll bite. What?
WALTER. I'm in love.

JIM. Aw, give me a break!
WALTER. I am!
JIM. I believe you. All right? But so what? Did you really have to ruin my shoes and break up my night to tell me that? So you're in love. I'm sure it seems very important to you, Walter, but really, get serious.
WALTER. You don't understand.
JIM. No doubt I don't.
WALTER. She's a mermaid.
JIM. What?
WALTER. She's a mermaid. The woman I'm in love with. She's a mermaid. And she lives in Central Park Lake.
JIM. In the lake.
WALTER. Yes.
JIM. Well, that makes sense. If she's a mermaid. That she would live in a lake. A fresh-water mermaid, huh?
WALTER. Don't make fun.
JIM. But it's so easy. What are we doing here?
WALTER. I want you to see her.
JIM. Why didn't you invite your parents so she could meet the family?
WALTER. I've seen her twice now. Always between two and two-thirty. (*Walter takes out a little plastic pumpkin.*)
JIM. What's that?
WALTER. A small plastic pumpkin.
JIM. Ask a silly question. (*Walter turns it on. It lights up.*) Oh, and it lights up! Very nice.
WALTER. It's our signal. I turn this on, and I call her name.
JIM. And how did you hit on this sophisticated system?
WALTER. It came to me in a dream, Jim.
JIM. A dream.
WALTER. Yeah. It's amazing how quickly you accept all these things once you've seen her.
JIM. I'll bet.
WALTER. Sally. Sally.
JIM. What are you saying?
WALTER. I'm calling her name.
JIM. Sally?
WALTER. That's right.
JIM. Sally the mermaid?
WALTER. That's right. Sally? Sally?

JIM. I'm leaving.

WALTER. No. Don't go. She should show up any minute. I want you to see her. I'm desperate for you to see her really. You see, I've always had a terrible longing in me. A color. A feeling. And I didn't know what it was. Now I do. I'm a man who loves a mermaid. And she loves me. And it's wonderful. But it's sad, too. It's really sad for a man to love a mermaid. You can see that? And it's even worse if it's a dream. To love somebody you can't have is bad enough. But to love somebody you can't have, and she's a dream, too . . . That's too sad. Do you know what I'm talking about, Jimmy? You're my best friend in the world. If you don't know what I'm talking about then there's nobody.

JIM. I don't know what the fuck you're talking about.

WALTER. Just wait a minute. Just one more minute. Sally? Sally? Please?

JIM. There's no one out there, Walter.

WALTER. She's out there. Sally?

JIM. No. There's nothing out there. Why don't you come with me? You should go home and get some sleep.

WALTER. No. No.

JIM. All right.

WALTER. 'Member back in the days when we saw everything the same way? And nothing was impossible? And we loved each other?

JIM. I'm worried about you, Walter.

WALTER. I'm okay.

JIM. No, you're not. You're not. (*Exit Jim.*)

WALTER. Sally, why didn't you come? He was my best friend. He was my friend. Sally? O God. Lonely. (*A ghostly woman's voice is heard. Light comes from the source of it, illuminating Walter's face.*)

SALLY. Walter! Walter!

WALTER. You've come!

SALLY. I love you!

WALTER. And I you. My solitary, unprovable, deepest only love.

FADEOUT

PROPERTY LIST

Small plastic pumpkin which lights up (Walter)

WELCOME TO THE MOON

WELCOME TO THE MOON

A lowdown Bronx bar. Vinnie, an Italian guy in his early thirties, is sitting on a stool, nursing a beer. Artie, the bartender, a wasted old Irishman, sits in the corner, reading the paper. Enter Stephen, gaunt, dark-eyed.

VINNIE. Steve?
STEPHEN. Vinnie! How are you?
VINNIE. Good! Good! How you been, man?
STEPHEN. Alright.
VINNIE. You look like shit. It's been three years, man. I've been sitting here counting.
STEPHEN. Too long.
VINNIE. Damn right it's too long. Artie, give Steve a beer. (*Artie silently does so.*)
STEPHEN. Thanks. So where is everybody? This used to be the big hangout.
VINNIE. Everybody split a long time since. The Bronx is dead.
STEPHEN. Where'd they all go?
VINNIE. Upstate.
STEPHEN. How come you didn't go?
VINNIE. Guess I'm lazy. Got the job at the Post Office. It's good. And I just don't like upstate. Fuckin' Poughkeepsie. Fuckin' Nanuet. Gimme a break.
STEPHEN. You like the Bronx.
VINNIE. That's right.
STEPHEN. I likc the Bronx, too.
VINNIE. Now that does not compute.
STEPHEN. What d'you mean?
VINNIE. You were the first one to go.
STEPHEN. It just worked out that way. I went in the army, and by the time I got out . . .
VINNIE. Yeah, I know. By the time you got out, time and tide had you by the balls, and you were on your way to who knows

where. Anyway, why would you come back to the Bronx? The Bronx is dead.

STEPHEN. There's still some neighborhoods that seem okay.

VINNIE. The Bronx is like one a those moon craters, man. Another couple of years, they're gonna be sendin astronauts up here. Guys from Houston 'ill be collecting rocks on Tremont Avenue. So how's Manhattan?

STEPHEN. Manhattan's all right. It's good. Exciting. Always a lot going on.

VINNIE. Uh-huh.

STEPHEN. Good museums.

VINNIE. Museums. Yeah, they're electrifying.

STEPHEN. I can walk to school.

VINNIE. Still in school! Ain't that some shit!

STEPHEN. Well, I wasn't in right along. There was the service. And then a lot of shitty jobs.

VINNIE. And then you got married.

STEPHEN. Yeah.

VINNIE. What is she again?

STEPHEN. A Speech Pathologist.

VINNIE. A Speech Pathologist. It sounds fuckin' hideous. I live with a Speech Pathologist.

STEPHEN. Very nice.

VINNIE. Sorry. I'm hungry. Artie, what do you got to eat?

ARTIE. Canadian bacon and cheese.

VINNIE. Gimme one. You want one?

STEPHEN. All right.

VINNIE. Two.

ARTIE. (*Puts sandwiches in a little oven.*) It'll take twelve minutes.

VINNIE. We're not going nowhere.

STEPHEN. Vinnie . . .

VINNIE. Yeah?

STEPHEN. Vinnie . . . It's good to see you, man. (*Starts to cry.*)

VINNIE. It's good to see you, too, man. Time goes by, and everybody goes away, and you see what you had.

STEPHEN. It's true.

VINNIE. You went out and stood on the corner, and everybody you ever knew was hanging there with you.

STEPHEN. You know . . .
VINNIE. It was your neighborhood. It was something to be inside of. You could do anything because you knew the fuckin' rules.
STEPHEN. You know, I think I left my wife.
VINNIE. What d'you mean, you think you left your wife?
STEPHEN. Things have been bad for a long time. I don't know why. School is driving me up the wall. I can't seem to . . . I can't seem to find . . . There's nothing left that I enjoy.
VINNIE. I'm sorry.
STEPHEN. Nothing happened. That's the really strange thing. I just told her I felt like going . . . coming to the Bronx, you know, the old neighborhood, and she said okay. And I walked out.
VINNIE. Don't sound final to me. You can go back.
STEPHEN. I don't think I can. I don't want to.
VINNIE. It's your life.
STEPHEN. We were . . . We're friends, Vinnie. I know I didn't call you for three years, and I know I didn't keep in touch much for years before that, but, we're friends.
VINNIE. Yeah.
STEPHEN. I don't really have any friends in Manhattan. I know people, but . . .
VINNIE. Shut up.
STEPHEN. Yeah.
VINNIE. Look, Steve. How do you feel?
STEPHEN. I'm all right.
VINNIE. Yeah?
STEPHEN. Yeah.
VINNIE. Cause when I got your call, I thought you might like to see some of the old crowd. So I phoned around. A couple of the folks should be here in a minute. Is that gonna be okay?
STEPHEN. Who?
VINNIE. Ronny.
STEPHEN. Ronny. Yeah, I'd like to see Ronny. How's he doing?
VINNIE. Bad. Ronny's always doing bad. Tried to kill himself.
STEPHEN. No!
VINNIE. Three times.
STEPHEN. Really?

VINNIE. Yeah. I make him come around. He comes to my house sometimes. A few beers. Whatever. To keep him from thinking.
STEPHEN. About what?
VINNIE. I don't know. But whenever he starts thinking about it, he goes right down the tubes.
STEPHEN. Who else?
VINNIE. Shirley.
STEPHEN. Shirley.
VINNIE. Shirley Dunbar.
STEPHEN. She's coming here?
VINNIE. Yeah. She should be here now.
STEPHEN. Bartender!
VINNIE. His name's Artie.
STEPHEN. Artie!
ARTIE. The sandwiches aren't ready yet. A little bell rings when the sandwiches are ready.
STEPHEN. Gimme a big glass of tequila.
VINNIE. What are you doing?
ARTIE. How many shots?
STEPHEN. Five.
VINNIE. Five!
ARTIE. Okay. One. Two. Three. Four. Five.
VINNIE. What are you doing?
STEPHEN. You don't know what you've done.
VINNIE. I guess not.
STEPHEN. Shirley's coming here.
VINNIE. So?
STEPHEN. You know she was my girlfriend.
VINNIE. She was your girlfriend when you were seventeen. Hey, you been seeing her on the sly?
STEPHEN. I haven't laid eyes on her since the day we broke up.
VINNIE. That was fourteen years ago.
STEPHEN. So?
VINNIE. So what are you doing?
STEPHEN. I'm trying to drink enough tequila to hold myself together.
VINNIE. What the hell are you talking about?
STEPHEN. Don't you understand? That's why my marriage is

breaking up! That's why I can't make it through college! That's why I can't gain any weight! Can't sleep! Can't . . . live. I'm still in love with Shirley Dunbar! (*Vinnie bursts out laughing.*)

VINNIE. You're kidding me?

STEPHEN. I can't joke about it.

VINNIE. But it was fourteen years ago!

STEPHEN. Five thousand, one hundred and twenty-three days ago.

VINNIE. Wow.

STEPHEN. The day we broke up, I knew it wasn't over. I knew we'd have to meet at least one more time. I was crying. I could see that she didn't understand, didn't want to understand. The thing we had was big. I joined the service to get away. I couldn't stand seeing her walking down the street, knowing that she wasn't mine anymore. That's why I never came back to live in the Bronx! That's why I hardly ever called you! Why I hardly ever called anybody from the old days. You were all part of that time, the time Shirley and I were together. The only time in my life I was ever really alive! (*Stephen downs the tequila at one toss, throws himself down on the bar, and begins to sob violently. The sandwich bell rings.*)

ARTIE. (*Serving sandwiches, apparently unfazed.*) Two canadian bacon and cheese. You want mustard with those? (*Getting no answer, he shrugs and goes back to his paper.*)

VINNIE. I am impressed. Here I thought you were just another nice shaky guy looking for his roots, and you turn out to be Heathcliff. "I cannot live without my love, I cannot die without my soul!" Welcome to the moon. (*Spots something outside.*) Oh shit. Steve, Ronny's coming down the block. I know it's a lot to ask, but can you pull yourself together? It's just that Ronny is real easy to get depressed, and he is always trying to do himself in, and . . . Can you hear me? (*Stephen's crying has continued unabated.*) Oh well. Fuck it. (*Ronny, a very short, very depressed guy, enters slowly. Without breaking rhythm, he joins Stephen at the bar, strikes the identical pose, and commences to sob with equal violence. A moment passes like this.*) You know what you two guys need? Canadian bacon and cheese. (*The two stop crying, take the sandwiches, and start to chew. There is an occasional whimper.*) You want some mustard? Artie, give them mustard. (*They take mustard from Artie.*) That's it.

RONNY. Hi, Steve.
STEPHEN. Hi, Ronny.
RONNY. Long time, no see.
STEPHEN. Yeah. How you been?
RONNY. Bad. Real bad.
STEPHEN. Me too.
RONNY. Artie. Gimme whatever Steve's drinking.
ARTIE. He's drinking five shots of tequila.
RONNY. All right! Give us a round.
ARTIE. One. Two. Three. Four. Five. One . . .
VINNIE. Hey, Artie, could you count to yourself!
ARTIE. Okay. (*Whispers.*) Two. Three. Four. Five.
VINNIE. Ronny, you shouldn't be drinking a drink like that. You know how you get.
RONNY. You're right, Vinnie. (*Drinks it down; then to Stephen.*) I'm an attempted suicide. I've tried to kill myself three times. First time, I tied my feet to this big rock, and jumped in the Bronx River. But the water was only two feet deep. I stood there all day. I thought maybe the pollution would kill me. Buncha Spanish kids came and made fun of me. I finally went home. Then last year, I cut my throat. Right there. But I had to stop because it hurt. The third time, I threw myself in front of the A train, but the fuckin' thing broke down before it got to me. Lately I've been eating in all the restaurants that have health violations. That might do it. Who knows? I've missed you, Steve. I wasn't much when you left, but I'm a total fuckin' disaster now.
STEPHEN. At least you've had the guts to . . . (*Starts to cry again.*)
RONNY. What's the matter with him?
VINNIE. He just left his wife.
RONNY. That's the mouth disease lady, right?
STEPHEN. Speech Pathologist! (*Goes back to crying.*)
RONNY. Right.
VINNIE. You ain't gonna believe this, but he's still in love with Shirley Dunbar!
RONNY. Really?
VINNIE. He's been in love with her for fourteen years without seeing her.
STEPHEN. I can see her in my mind! (*Goes back to crying.*)

RONNY. Sure you can, man! Sure you can! I know what's the matter with him, Vinnie, and it's real bad.
VINNIE. What?
RONNY. He's obsessed, man! He's got his fuckin' self an obsession.
VINNIE. How do you know?
RONNY. I know. I want you to do me a favor, Vin. I want you to give me five minutes with him. Take a walk around the block. I can help him. I know about this.
VINNIE. You do?
RONNY. Yeah.
VINNIE. But Shirley's coming. I invited her. She should be here any minute.
RONNY. All the more reason, man. Gimme five minutes right now, before she gets here, to straighten him out. I can do it, Vinnie. Gimme the chance!
VINNIE. Alright. (*To Steve.*) I'm going out for a few minutes, okay? (*Steve nods through his tears. Exit Vinnie.*)
RONNY. Steve! Steve! You gotta listen to me, Steve. There isn't much time. I know how you feel. You love Shirley, right? Shirley don't love you, right? It's a tragedy, right? You don't have to tell me. I know it's a tragedy. I know . . . cause I got the same thing. I'm gonna tell you what I've never told anybody. And you gotta understand quick cause there's no time! I'm in love with Vinnie. That's right! And I always have been. But I know it can't work so I never told him. That's why I'm a suicide attempt. Because my life is ruined from loving someone who don't love me.
STEPHEN. Me too.
RONNY. I know! I know! And that's why I want you to commit suicide with me.
STEPHEN. You do?
RONNY. It's perfect! We both kill ourselves right now, and then they find us. The two idiots who are responsible! Will you do it?
STEPHEN. How?
RONNY. A really good way. Plastic bags. (*Pulls two plastic bags with drawstrings out of his jacket.*) We just put these over our heads and die.
STEPHEN. How long will it take?

RONNY. Not long! How much air could be in a little plastic bag?

STEPHEN. All right, I'll do it!

RONNY. (*Handing him a bag.*) We ain't got much time. We'll die quicker if we do exercise. That makes you breathe faster. (*Ronny and Stephen don their bags, and do jumping jacks. Then they run up and down the length of the bar. Ronny urges Stephen along, shouting "Faster" and "Run" and such. They both grow weak.*) This is it! This is it! (*Ronny lays down on the bar, and Stephen lays down on the floor. Artie watches all this without concern. Enter Shirley, blond, a little plump, big round eyes. She takes it all in and screams.*)

SHIRLEY. They got bags on their heads! (*Enter Vinnie.*) Everybody's got bags on their heads!

ARTIE. I don't have a bag on my head. (*Vinnie rips the bags off their heads. They are both a little dazed, but otherwise fine.*)

VINNIE. That was very immature, Ronny.

RONNY. Four times.

VINNIE. And Steve, I'm surprised at you.

RONNY. Four times.

STEPHEN. It really seemed like the right thing to do.

SHIRLEY. Is that you, Stephen?

STEPHEN. Shirley?

SHIRLEY. Hi.

STEPHEN. Hi. My hair's all messed up.

SHIRLEY. That's all right.

VINNIE. (*To Ronny.*) Are you okay?

RONNY. Yeah.

VINNIE. Why do you keep trying to kill yourself, Ronny?

RONNY. Do you really wanna know?

STEPHEN. You look great.

SHIRLEY. You too. You got great color.

STEPHEN. That's cause I was suffocating.

SHIRLEY. Oh.

RONNY. I'm in love with you.

VINNIE. You're what?

SHIRLEY. Did you hear what he said?

RONNY. I'm in love with you.

SHIRLEY. He said it again.

VINNIE. That's impossible.

SHIRLEY. Oh my God, he's a faggot!

STEPHEN. Shirley, I love you.
SHIRLEY. I never woulda guessed it! I knew Ronny was crazy, but a crazy faggot?
RONNY. I loved you ever since we were little boys. On the seesaw. Playing curb ball. I never said nothing cause I knew it would hurt your feelings and you wouldn't like me anymore. I figured it was easier just to kill myself.
VINNIE. I don't know what to say.
RONNY. What could you say?
VINNIE. I love you . . . too?
SHIRLEY. Oh my God, Vinnie's a faggot, too!
RONNY. You what?
VINNIE. I guess I love you, too.
SHIRLEY. And they're brazen! They're brazen faggots!
RONNY. Why didn't you ever say anything?
VINNIE. Why didn't you?
RONNY, VINNIE. I was afraid.
STEPHEN. Shirley.
SHIRLEY. You are straight, right?
STEPHEN. Yeah, I'm straight.
SHIRLEY. That's a relief.
STEPHEN. Shirley, I love you.
SHIRLEY. You do?
STEPHEN. Yes.
SHIRLEY. Still?
STEPHEN. Yes.
SHIRLEY. Why?
STEPHEN. I don't know.
SHIRLEY. It's been about a hundred years now you've been loving me.
STEPHEN. I know.
SHIRLEY. And I've never loved you.
STEPHEN. I know.
SHIRLEY. The old crowd's together again.
STEPHEN. Yes. (*Artie sings "When You Were Sweet Sixteen." He has a lovely tenor. The two couples look into each others' eyes with sweet sadness.*)
ARTIE. (*Singing.*) When first I saw the love light in your eyes
I dreamt the world held nought but joy for me
And even though we've drifted far apart

I never dream but that I dream of thee
I love you as I never loved before
When first I saw you on the village green
Come to me 'ere this dream of life is o'er
I love as I loved you when you were sweet
When you were sweet
Sixteen
(*The lights go down.*)

THE END

PROPERTY LIST

Bar
Bar stools
Bottles of beer
Newspaper (Artie)
Toaster oven, with sandwiches
Bottle of tequila
Glasses
Jar of mustard
Plastic bags (2) with drawstrings (Ronny)

NEW PLAYS

• **SMASH by Jeffrey Hatcher.** Based on the novel, AN UNSOCIAL SOCIALIST by George Bernard Shaw, the story centers on a millionaire Socialist who leaves his bride on their wedding day because he fears his passion for her will get in the way of his plans to overthrow the British government. *"SMASH is witty, cunning, intelligent, and skillful."* –*Seattle Weekly.* *"SMASH is a wonderfully high-style British comedy of manners that evokes the world of Shaw's high-minded heroes and heroines, but shaped by a post modern sensibility."* –*Seattle Herald.* [5M, 5W] ISBN: 0-8222-1553-5

• **PRIVATE EYES by Steven Dietz.** A comedy of suspicion in which nothing is ever quite what it seems. *"Steven Dietz's ... Pirandellian smooch to the mercurial nature of theatrical illusion and romantic truth, Dietz's spiraling structure and breathless pacing provide enough of an oxygen rush to revive any moribund audience member ... Dietz's mastery of playmaking ... is cause for kudos."* –*The Village Voice.* *"The cleverest and most artful piece presented at the 21st annual [Humana] festival was PRIVATE EYES by writer-director Steven Dietz."* –*The Chicago Tribune.* [3M, 2W] ISBN: 0-8222-1619-1

• **DIMLY PERCEIVED THREATS TO THE SYSTEM by Jon Klein.** Reality and fantasy overlap with hilarious results as this unforgettable family attempts to survive the nineties. *"Here's a play whose point about fractured families goes to the heart, mind -- and ears."* –*The Washington Post.* *" ... an end-of-the millennium comedy about a family on the verge of a nervous breakdown ... Trenchant and hilarious ... "* –*The Baltimore Sun.* [2M, 4W] ISBN: 0-8222-1677-9

• **HONOUR by Joanna Murray-Smith.** In a series of intense confrontations, a wife, husband, lover and daughter negotiate the forces of passion, lust, history, responsibility and honour. *"Tight, crackling dialogue (usually played out in punchy verbal duels) captures characters unable to deal with emotions ... Murray-Smith effectively places her characters in situations that strip away pretense."* –*Variety.* *"HONOUR might just capture a few honors of its own."* –*Time Out Magazine.* [1M, 3W] ISBN: 0-8222-1683-3

• **NINE ARMENIANS by Leslie Ayvazian.** A revealing portrait of three generations of an Armenian-American family. *" ... Ayvazian's obvious personal exploration ... is evocative, and her picture of an American Life colored nostalgically by an increasingly alien ethnic tradition, is persuasively embedded into a script of a certain supple grace ... "* –*The NY Post.* *"... NINE ARMENIANS is a warm, likable work that benefits from ... Ayvazian's clear-headed insight into the dynamics of a close-knit family ... "* –*Variety.* [5M, 5W] ISBN: 0-8222-1602-7

• **PSYCHOPATHIA SEXUALIS by John Patrick Shanley.** Fetishes and psychiatry abound in this scathing comedy about a man and his father's argyle socks. *"John Patrick Shanley's new play, PSYCHOPATHIA SEXUALIS is ... perfectly poised between daffy comedy and believable human neurosis which Shanley combines so well ... "* –*The LA Times.* *"John Patrick Shanley's PSYCHOPATHIA SEXUALIS is a salty boulevard comedy with a bittersweet theme ... "* –*New York Magazine.* *"A tour de force of witty, barbed dialogue."* –*Variety.* [3M, 2W] ISBN: 0-8222-1615-9

DRAMATISTS PLAY SERVICE, INC.
440 Park Avenue South, New York, NY 10016 212-683-8960 Fax 212-213-1539
postmaster@dramatists.com www.dramatists.com

NEW PLAYS

• **A QUESTION OF MERCY by David Rabe.** The Obie Award-winning playwright probes the sensitive and controversial issue of doctor-assisted suicide in the age of AIDS in this poignant drama. *"There are many devastating ironies in Mr. Rabe's beautifully considered, piercingly clear-eyed work ..." –The NY Times. "With unsettling candor and disturbing insight, the play arouses pity and understanding of a troubling subject ... Rabe's provocative tale is an affirmation of dignity that rings clear and true." –Variety.* [6M, 1W] ISBN: 0-8222-1643-4

• **A DOLL'S HOUSE by Henrik Ibsen, adapted by Frank McGuinness. Winner of the 1997 Tony Award for best revival.** *"New, raw, gut-twisting and gripping. Easily the hottest drama this season." –USA Today. "Bold, brilliant and alive." –The Wall Street Journal. "A thunderclap of an evening that takes your breath away." –Time. "The stuff of Broadway legend." –Associated Press.* [4M, 4W, 2 boys] ISBN: 0-8222-1636-1

• **THE WAITING ROOM by Lisa Loomer.** Three women from different centuries meet in a doctor's waiting room in this dark comedy about the timeless quest for beauty -- and its cost. *"... THE WAITING ROOM ... is a bold, risky melange of conflicting elements that is ... terrifically moving ... There's no resisting the fierce emotional pull of the play." – The NY Times. " ... one of the high points of this year's Off-Broadway season ... THE WAITING ROOM is well worth a visit." –Back Stage.* [7M, 4W, flexible casting] ISBN: 0-8222-1594-2

• **MR. PETERS' CONNECTIONS by Arthur Miller.** Mr. Miller describes the protagonist as existing in a dream-like state when the mind is "freed to roam from real memories to conjectures, from trivialities to tragic insights, from terror of death to glorying in one's being alive." With this memory play, the Tony Award and Pulitzer Prize-winner reaffirms his stature as the world's foremost dramatist. *" ... a cross between Joycean stream-of-consciousness and Strindberg's dream plays, sweetened with a dose of William Saroyan's philosophical whimsy ... CONNECTIONS is most intriguing ... Miller scholars will surely find many connections of their own to make between this work and the author's earlier plays." –The NY Times.* [5M, 3W] ISBN: 0-8222-1687-6

• **THE STEWARD OF CHRISTENDOM by Sebastian Barry.** A freely imagined portrait of the author's great-grandfather, the last Chief Superintendent of the Dublin Metropolitan Police. *"MAGNIFICENT ... the cool, elegiac eye of James Joyce's THE DEAD; the bleak absurdity of Samuel Beckett's lost, primal characters; the cosmic anger of KING LEAR ..." –The NY Times. "Sebastian Barry's compassionate imaging of an ancestor he never knew is among the most poignant onstage displays of humanity in recent memory." –Variety.* [5M, 4W] ISBN: 0-8222-1609-4

• **SYMPATHETIC MAGIC by Lanford Wilson. Winner of the 1997 Obie for best play.** The mysteries of the universe, and of human and artistic creation, are explored in this award-winning play. *"Lanford Wilson's idiosyncratic SYMPATHETIC MAGIC is his BEST PLAY YET ... the rare play you WANT ... chock-full of ideas, incidents, witty or poetic lines, scientific and philosophical argument ... you'll find your intellectual faculties racing." – New York Magazine. "The script is like a fully notated score, next to which most new plays are cursory lead sheets." –The Village Voice.* [5M, 3W] ISBN: 0-8222-1630-2